PIANO SOLO

David Lanz
Cristofori's Dream... Re-Envisioned

- 6   CRISTOFORI'S DREAM
- 15   SPIRAL DANCE
- 28   GREEN INTO GOLD
- 40   WINGS TO ALTAIR
- 47   SUMMER'S CHILD
- 54   FREE FALL
- 63   A WHITER SHADE OF PALE
- 70   SEOUL IMPROVISATION

For more information on the *Cristofori's Dream... Re-Envisioned* album, visit **DavidLanz.com**

Cover photography by Rosanne Olson **rosanneolson.com**
Colmar Ruckers harpsichord provided by Nicholas Bunning
Art Direction by Daniela Boifava **visiongate.com**
Special thanks to Kathy Parsons **MainlyPiano.com**

ISBN 978-1-4768-7133-2

7777 W. BLUEMOUND RD. P.O. BOX 13819 MILWAUKEE, WI 53213

For all works contained herein:
Unauthorized copying, arranging, adapting, recording, Internet posting, public performance,
or other distribution of the printed music in this publication is an infringement of copyright.
Infringers are liable under the law.

Visit Hal Leonard Online at
www.halleonard.com

Re-Envisioning the Dream...

It is nearly impossible for me to wrap my head around the fact that twenty-five years have transpired since the release of the *Cristofori's Dream* recording and over twenty years since it appeared in my first Hal Leonard songbook, *Solos For New Age Piano*.

The spark, the divine seed if you will for *Cristofori's Dream*, was found in Judith Oringer's book, *Passion for the Piano*, a gift received from a good friend, and a very fortuitous gift it turned out to be!

In the forward of this book about the piano and various pianists throughout history, I read a dedication to a 16th century historical figure I had never heard of, a one, Bartolomeo Cristofori, "...the inventor of the piano." Never in my life had I stopped to think that the piano had an inventor, and I was completely taken off guard!

Immediately upon seeing the name Cristofori, my imagination mimicked the name and whispered in my mind, "Christ-Euphoria," followed directly by the title, "Cristofori's Dream." This was a defining moment! It was also highly unusual for me, as song titles rarely appear like this, if ever, or precede a composition, almost always coming to me during or even after a piece has been composed.

I don't ever recall having such strong feelings of gratitude come over me as I composed the title piece. "God bless Cristofori," I said to myself, "What would our world be like? What would my world be like without the piano?"

The goal for the twenty-fifth anniversary solo piano edition and this new companion songbook was to capture the essence of the original, but with the intimacy, spontaneity, and the sense of space afforded in a solo piano rendition.

The title track is transcribed as it was composed, but many of the other pieces have been opened up leaving room for improvisation and slight variations.

And I would once again like to say, as I did in the original 1988 liner notes, "This is dedicated to Bartolomeo Cristofori (1655-1731), the inventor of the piano—may his Dream live forever."

David Lanz

SONG DESCRIPTIONS

I have explained the origins of the title track, but every song has a story to tell. Here is a bit more of the background and the thought process used in creating the other pieces, which follow the title track in sequence.

SPIRAL DANCE

I once read an account by a fan saying that the song, "Spiral Dance," reminded her of an imagined playful twisting of a DNA's double helix. For me, it was simply the shape of its repeated musical phrases and the 6/8 time signature giving both its lilt, and its gentle dance rhythm.

GREEN INTO GOLD

Upon my first meeting in 1984 with John Morey, the president of Narada Records, he encouraged me to also try composing longer form pieces in contrast to what I had recorded on my first album *Heartsounds*, where several of the songs were just over two minutes in length. The result was "Green Into Gold," clocking in at nearly ten minutes on the original recording! The title was meant to convey the progression from spring (green) into fall (gold).

WINGS TO ALTAIR

It has been said that ancient peoples, especially sailors, relied on the bright star, Altair, for their navigational purposes. Altair has also been associated with the inner light of consciousness, or that of the third eye, which is helpful when traversing the inner realms. "Wings To Altair" is a musical journey that wishes to take the listener towards the destination of the latter.

SUMMER'S CHILD

Two summer's prior to the 1988 album's release, I had begun composing music inspired by my then one year old baby boy, Michael David. Watching him through the large picture window of our living room, as he played in our backyard in the warm August sun, I sat and composed "Summer's Child" right there at the same small spinet piano I had begun lessons on as a child in the 1950's. It would be sometime still before we could afford the beautiful grand piano that now graces our home. The success of *Cristofori's Dream* made that possible!

FREE FALL

The second to last song on the original recording stands out in my mind for two reasons. One, it was a piece that happily marked the end of a long writer's block. It was as if I was in a free fall at that time and this piece happily lifted me up just before I hit the ground!

Secondly, it was the only song on the original album not recorded on an acoustic piano. "Free Fall" was composed and then sequenced and recorded on a Yamaha DX7, a keyboard I used quite frequently in the studio back in the 1980's. On this new rendition for acoustic piano it has been rendered in a slightly more improvised fashion.

A WHITER SHADE OF PALE

There are 88 notes on the piano, and those 88's lined up for the release of the first single on *Cristofori's Dream*, "A Whiter Shade Of Pale," which hit the streets and the airwaves on 8/8/88!

At first there was a bit of controversy at my record label as to whether a so-called "New Age" musician should record a cover song, which might be viewed as too commercial and beneath the artistic purity of this new emerging genre of music. The controversy was short lived, and my remake of Procol Harum's classic "Summer Of Love" hit helped create a bridge between New Age and pop instrumental music and launched the album successfully at radio and straight up the charts!

SEOUL IMPROVISATION

While touring Korea in September of 2010 I chose, spur of the moment, to end one of my evening's concert performances with a heart-felt solo piano improvisation. This piece is a musical "thank you" for the tremendous support the Korean people have given me and my music over the many years and this is its first printed transcription.

"A Whiter Shade Of Pale" was the finale on the original 1988 release, but I felt that this improvisation was a fitting end to this re-envisioned edition, as it also sprung like a dream, from a place of heart-felt gratitude.

The Cristofori's Dream Story...

As the music begins we find our selves in a small picturesque 16th century Italian village. The sun has set and in the dusky sky, stars are just appearing. Looking through a leaded glass window, candlelight flickering within, we faintly see harpsichord maker Bartolomeo Cristofori engrossed in his work.

It has been a rather tedious and frustrating day for Cristofori, again putting in long hours, hoping for a breakthrough with his new invention; an invention, that will eventually transform the harpsichord into his imagined pianoforte.

With the day's work done, Cristofori puts tools aside, blows out the candle on his workbench, lays his head down, and falls asleep.

As slumber over takes him, he begins to dream; the music continues and two beautiful luminous goddesses appear. Through an impressionistic dance, Cristofori is shown the evolution his invention will go through in the next several hundred years and is given a sense of the tremendous impact the piano will have on the world of music.

...as told in concert by David Lanz

Majestically, the piece keeps building as the dream unfolds. The goddesses fade from view and he suddenly finds himself standing in a balcony overlooking a magnificent opera house. At center stage is a nine-foot concert grand piano and a full symphony orchestra; playing one final chorus they crescendo together, reach a musical peak, and then everything begins to spin and spiral downward. The dream vanishes.

From here the music softens, and Cristofori awakes. He is so inspired by this vision, that even though it is still the middle of the night, he relights his candle, reaches for his tools, and goes back to work.

Now the piece slowly begins to wind down much like a child's music box, and as the very last chord of the song sounds...Cristofori's harpsichord...changes magically into a piano...*Cristofori's Dream*.

CRISTOFORI'S DREAM

By DAVID LANZ

© 1988 NARA MUSIC (BMI)
Admin. at EMICMGPUBLISHING.COM
All Rights Reserved Used by Permission

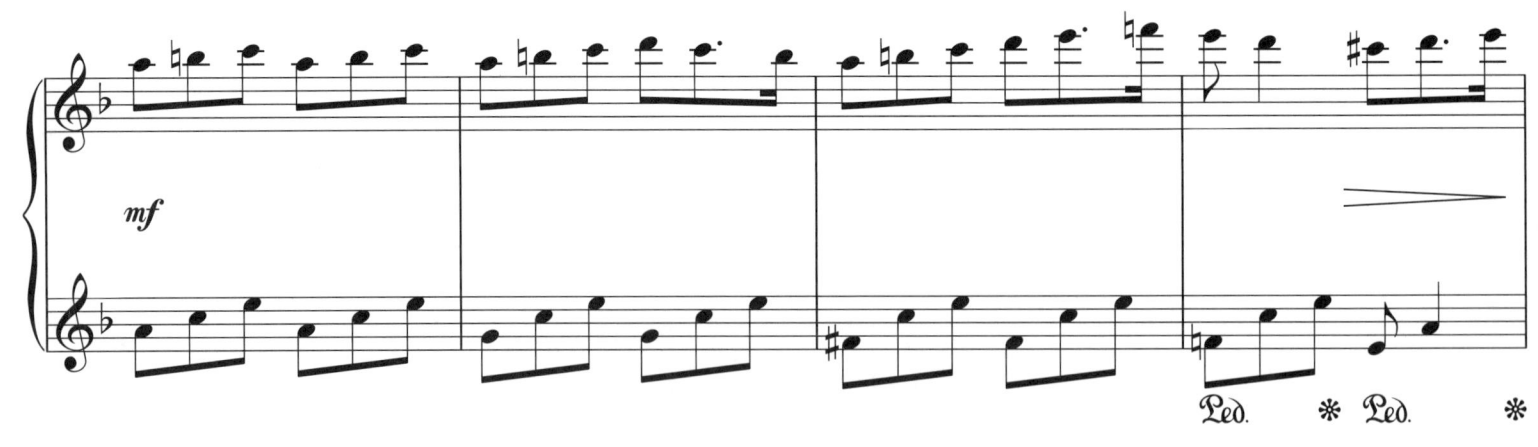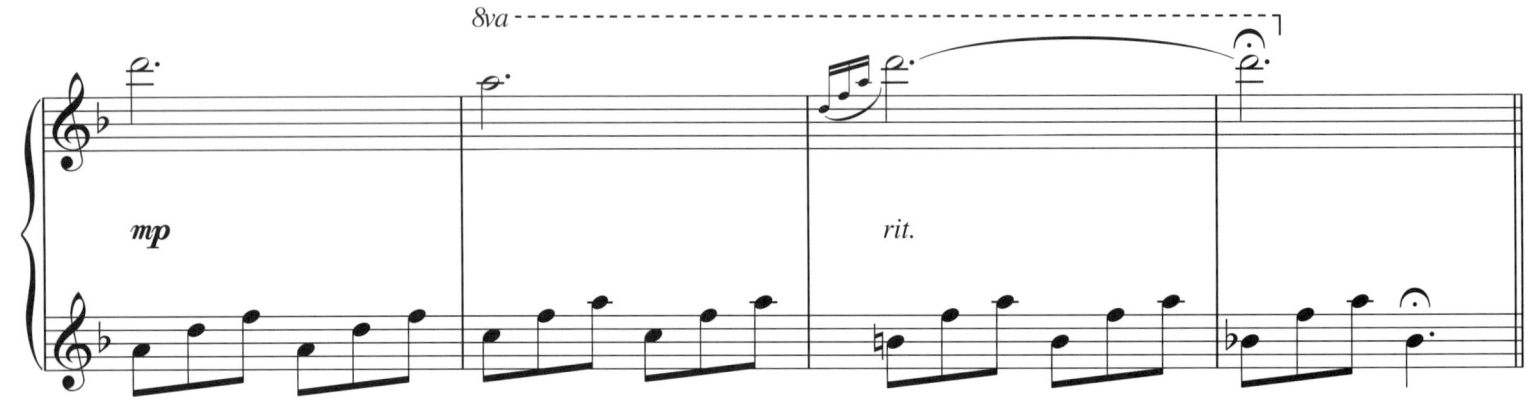

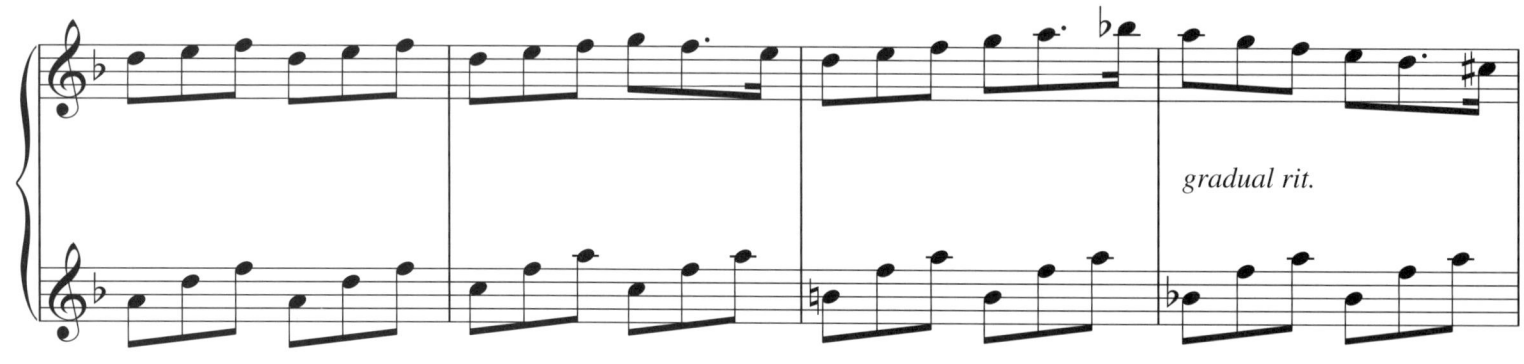

SPIRAL DANCE

By DAVID LANZ

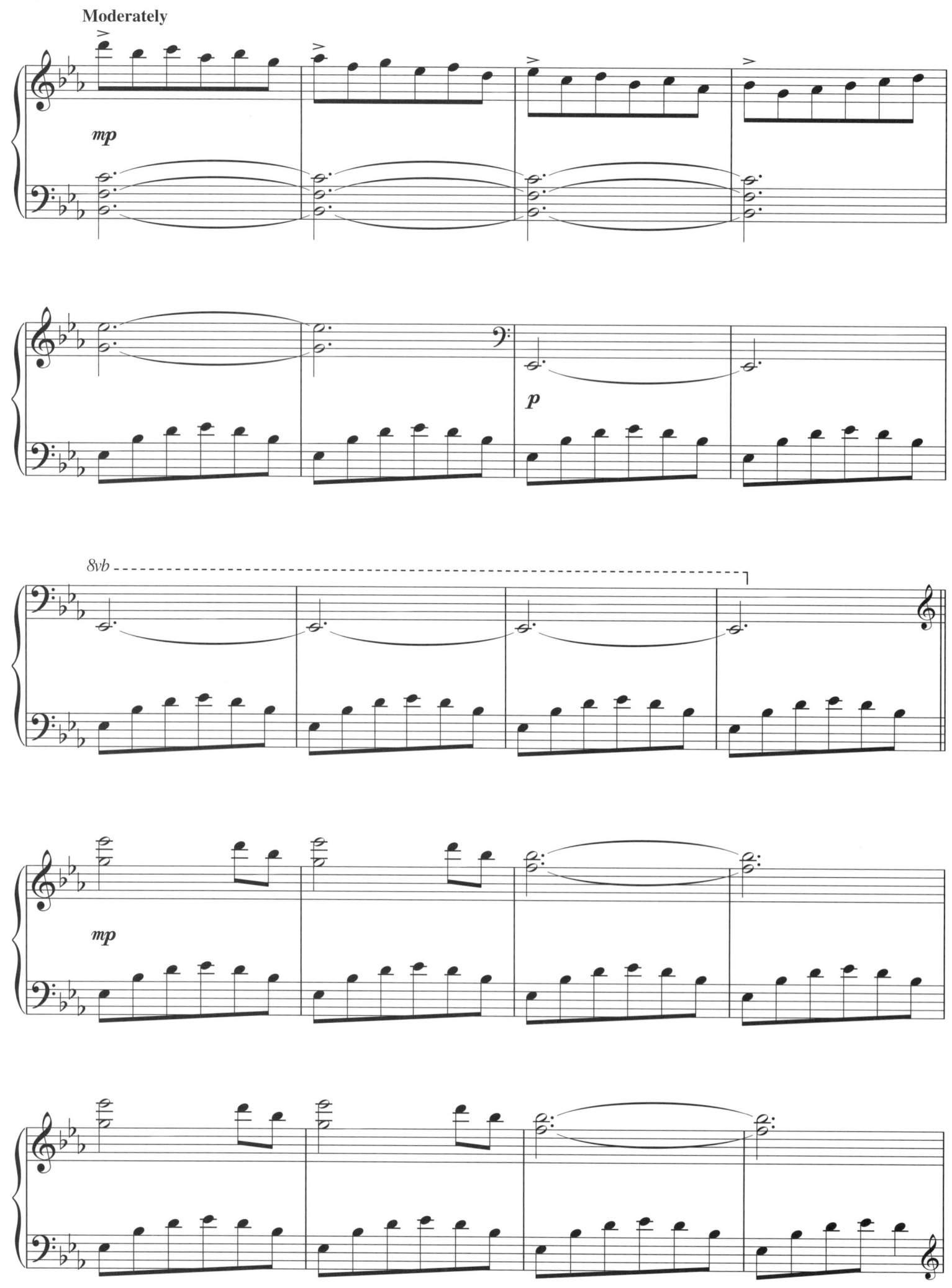

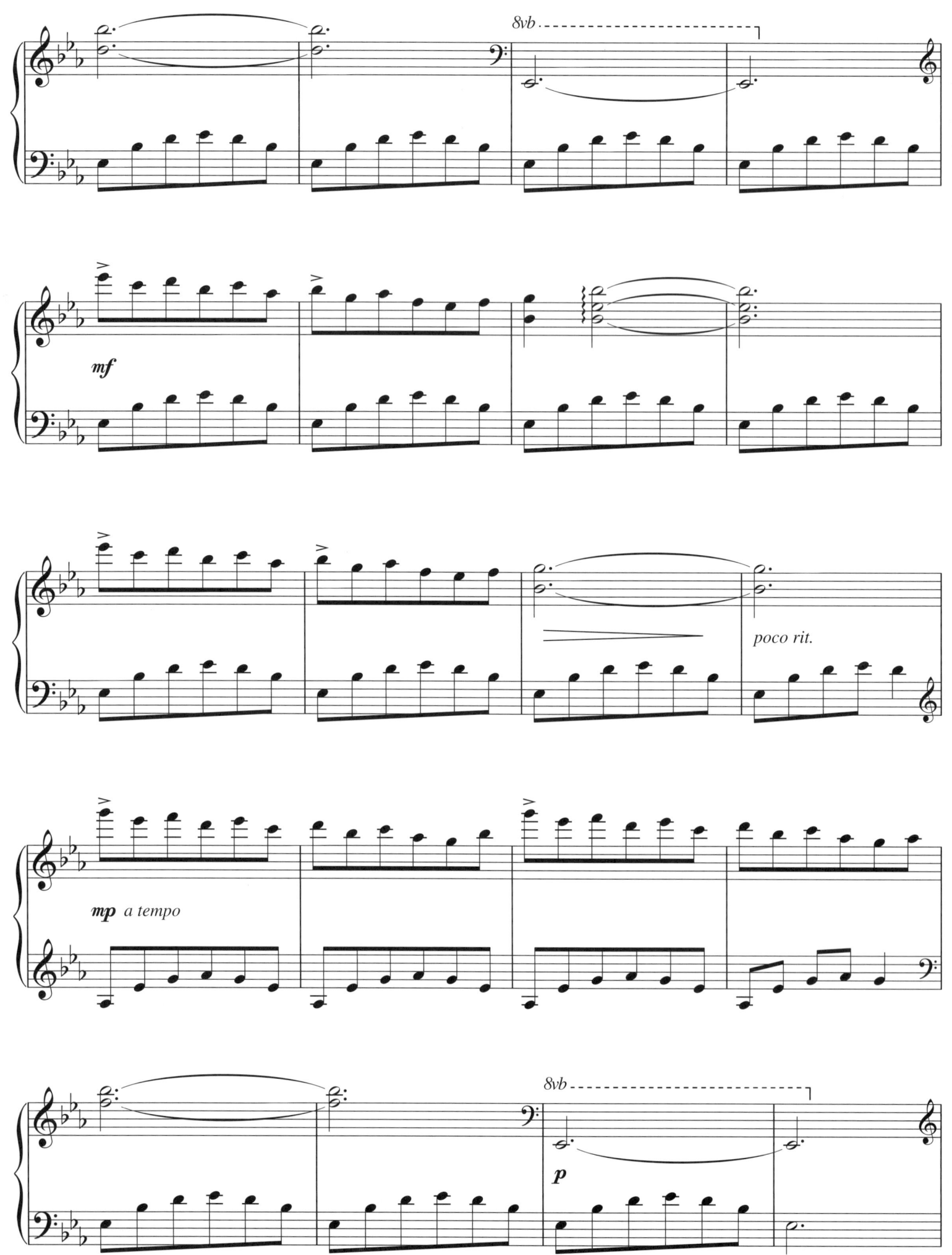

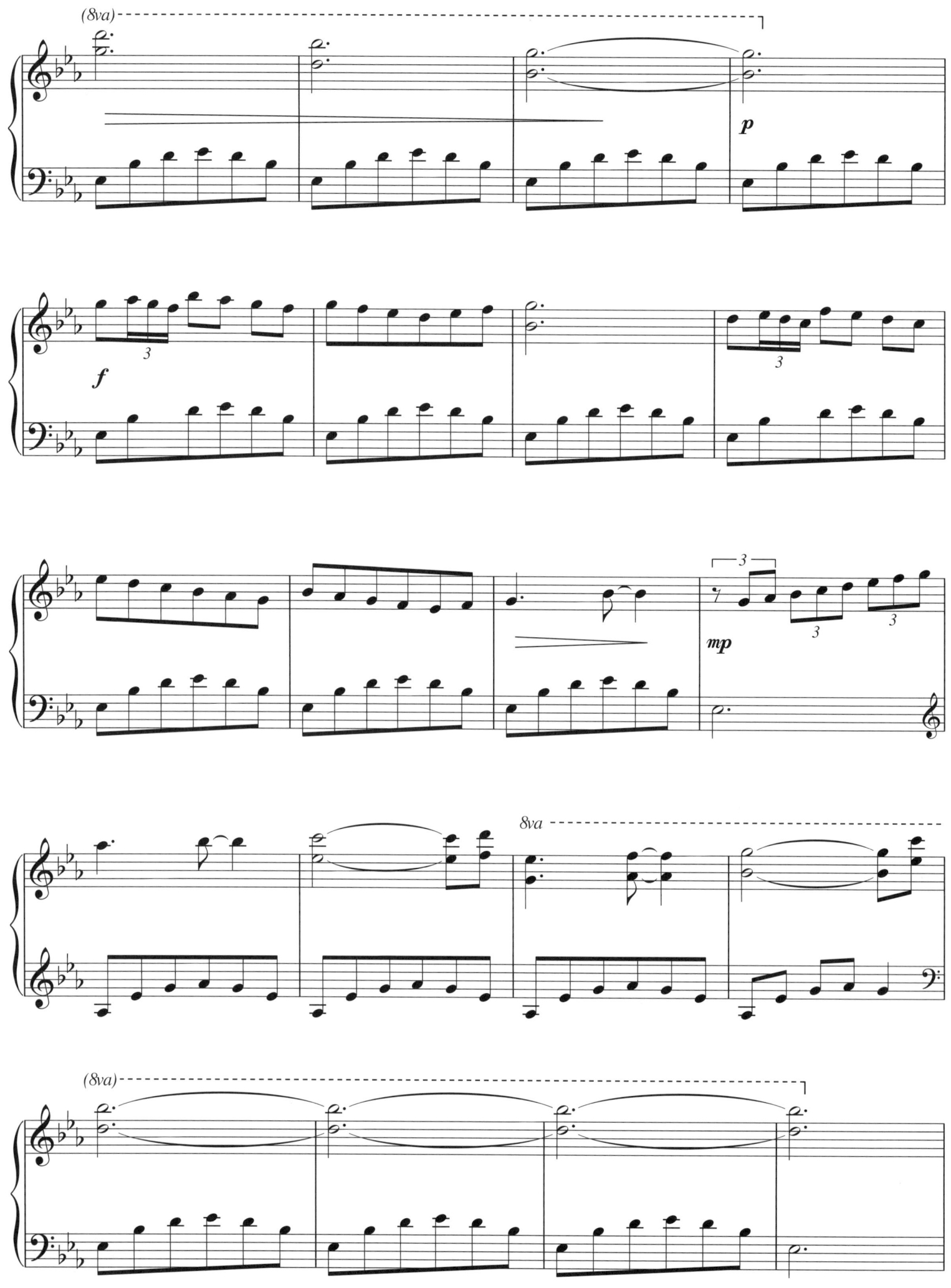

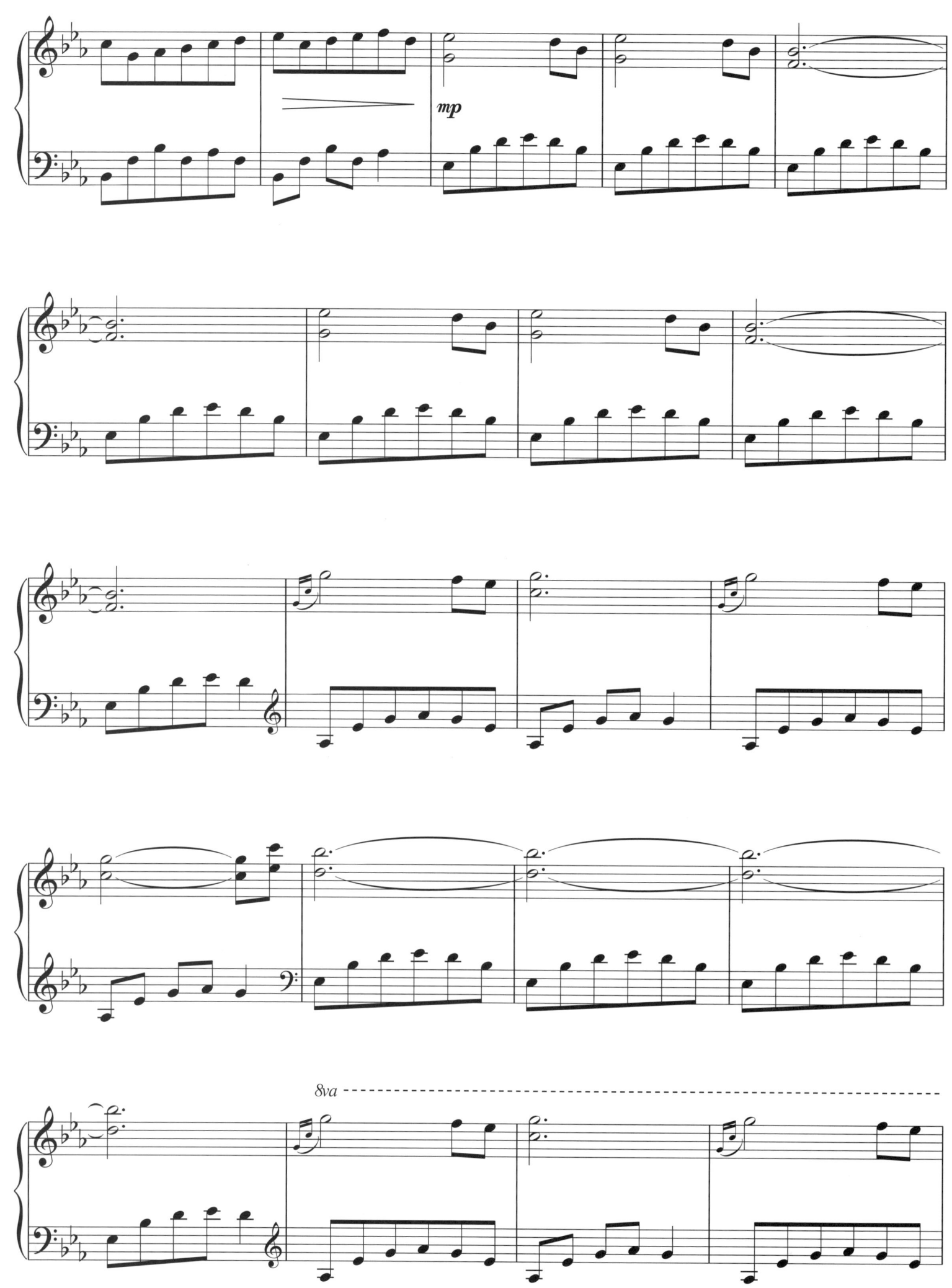

GREEN INTO GOLD

By DAVID LANZ

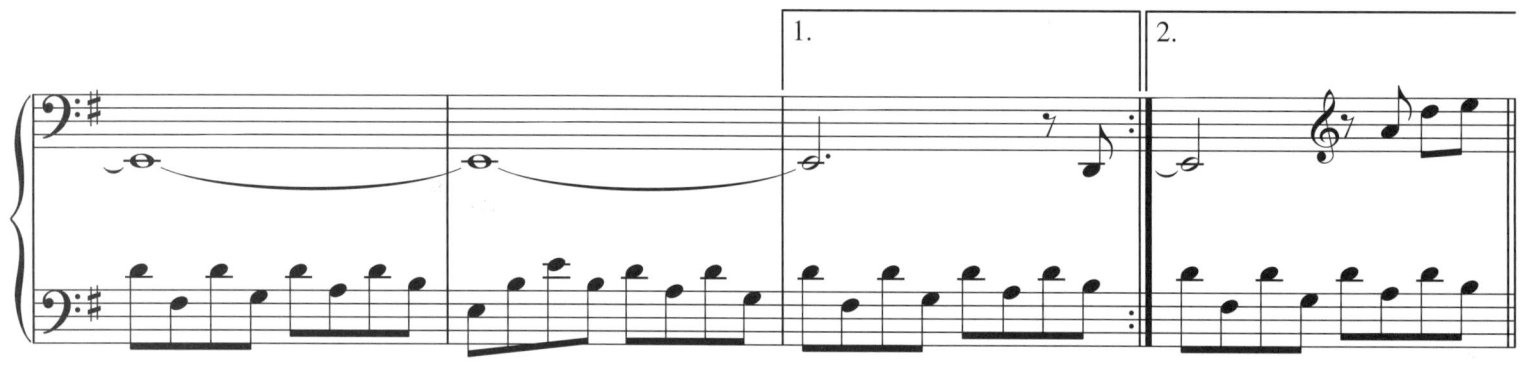
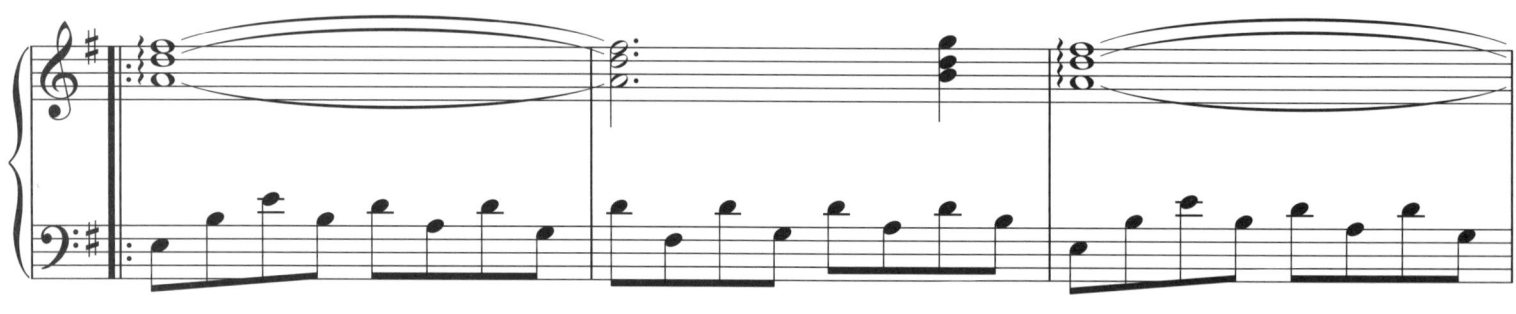

© 1988 NARA MUSIC (BMI)
Admin. at EMICMGPUBLISHING.COM
All Rights Reserved Used by Permission

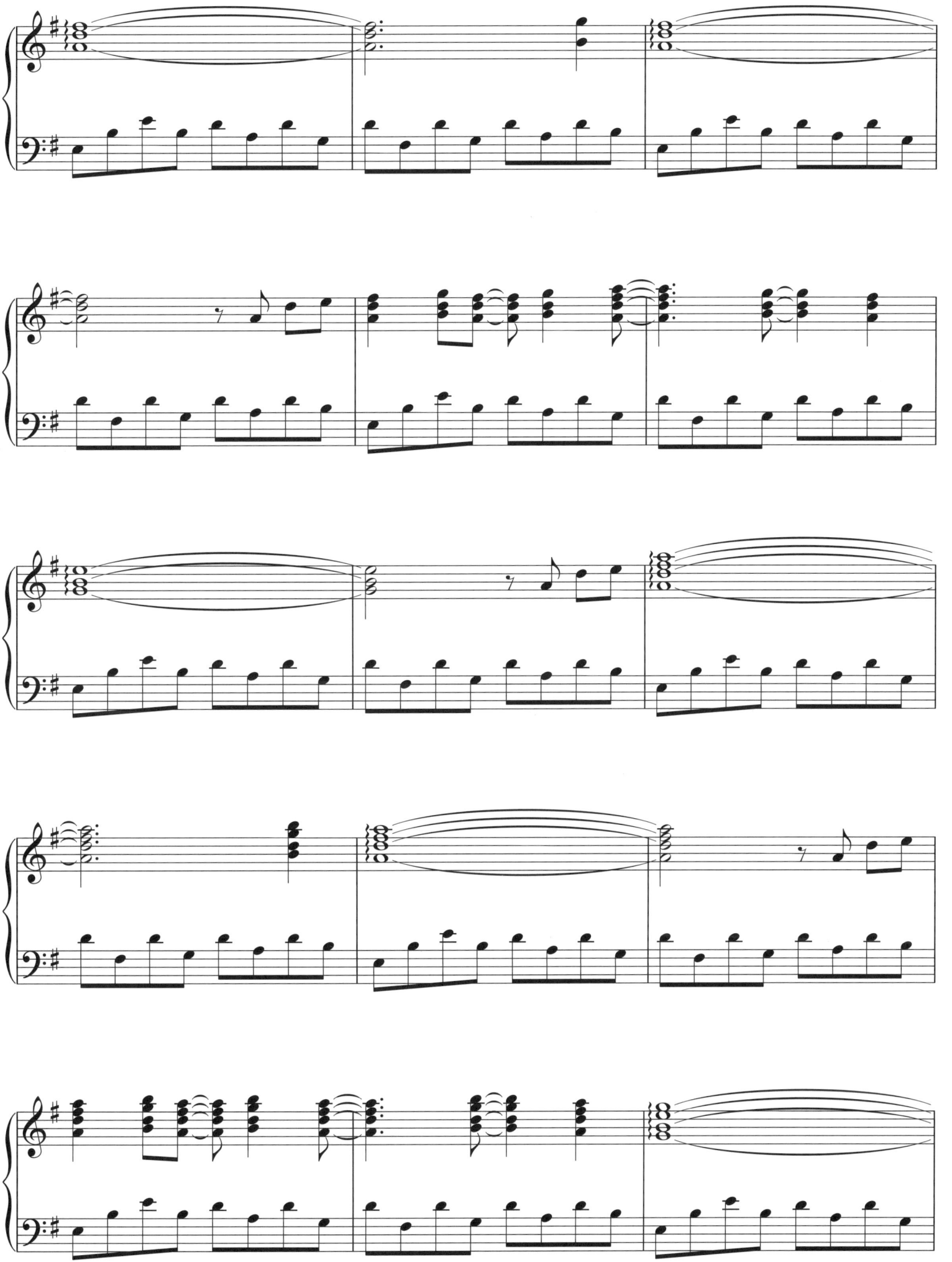

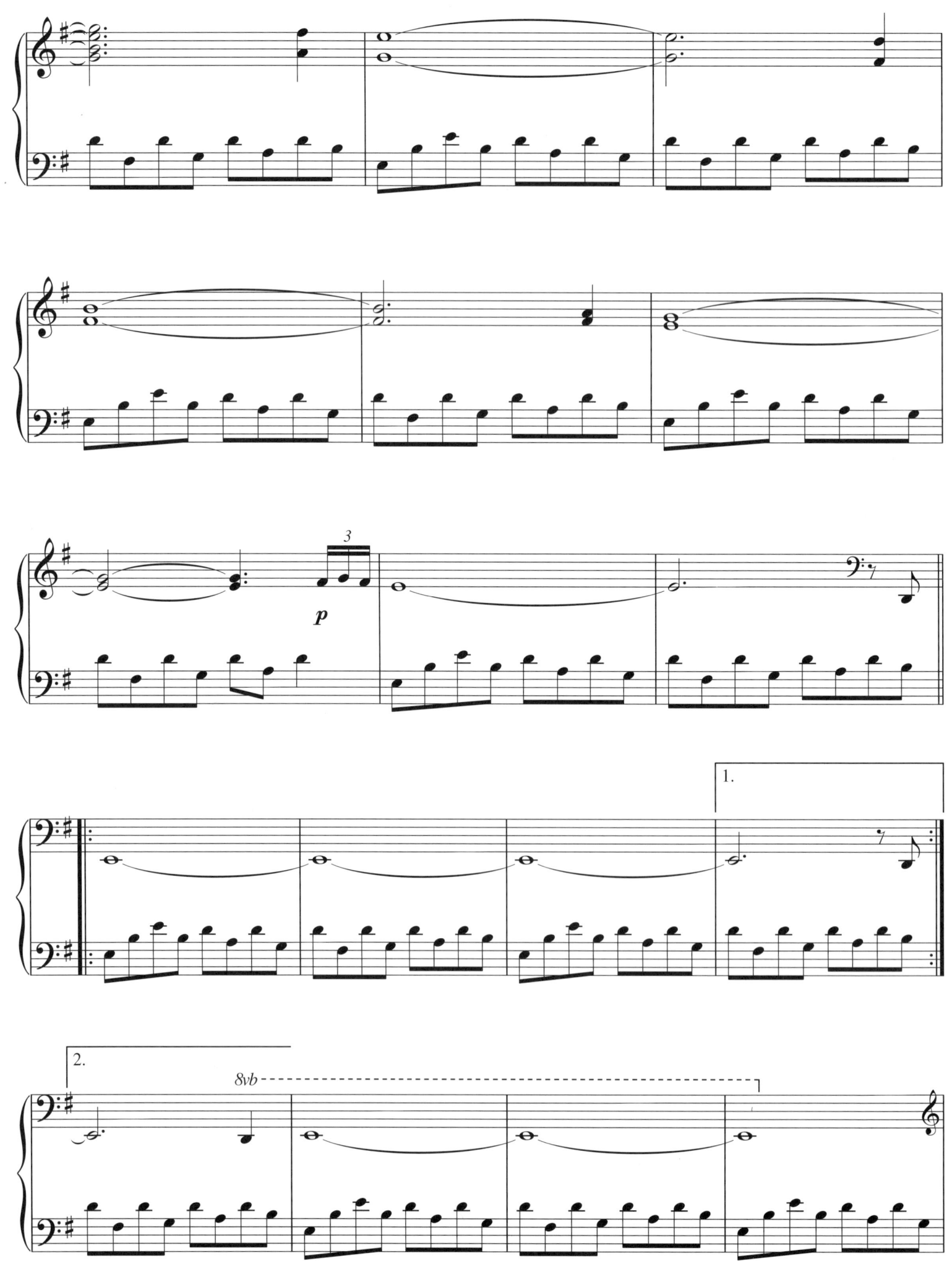

WINGS TO ALTAIR

By DAVID LANZ

Very freely, slowly

Pedal ad lib. throughout

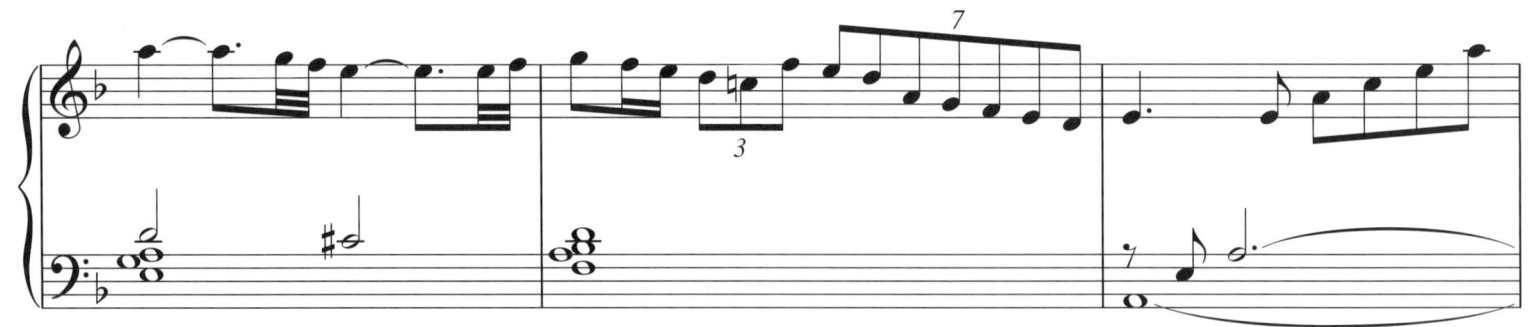

Moderately slow, steadily

© 1988 NARA MUSIC (BMI)
Admin. at EMICMGPUBLISHING.COM
All Rights Reserved   Used by Permission

SUMMER'S CHILD

By DAVID LANZ

* Pianists with smaller hands may roll the L.H. chords, remove a note, or play top notes with R.H.

© 1988 NARA MUSIC (BMI)
Admin. at EMICMGPUBLISHING.COM
All Rights Reserved   Used by Permission

FREE FALL

By DAVID LANZ

A WHITER SHADE OF PALE

Words and Music by KEITH REID,
GARY BROOKER and MATTHEW FISHER

* Pianists with smaller hands may roll the L.H. chords, remove a note, or play top notes with R.H.

© Copyright 1967 (Renewed) Onward Music Ltd., London, England
TRO - Essex Music, Inc., New York, controls all publication rights for the U.S.A. and Canada
International Copyright Secured
All Rights Reserved Including Public Performance For Profit
Used by Permission

SEOUL IMPROVISATION

By DAVID LANZ

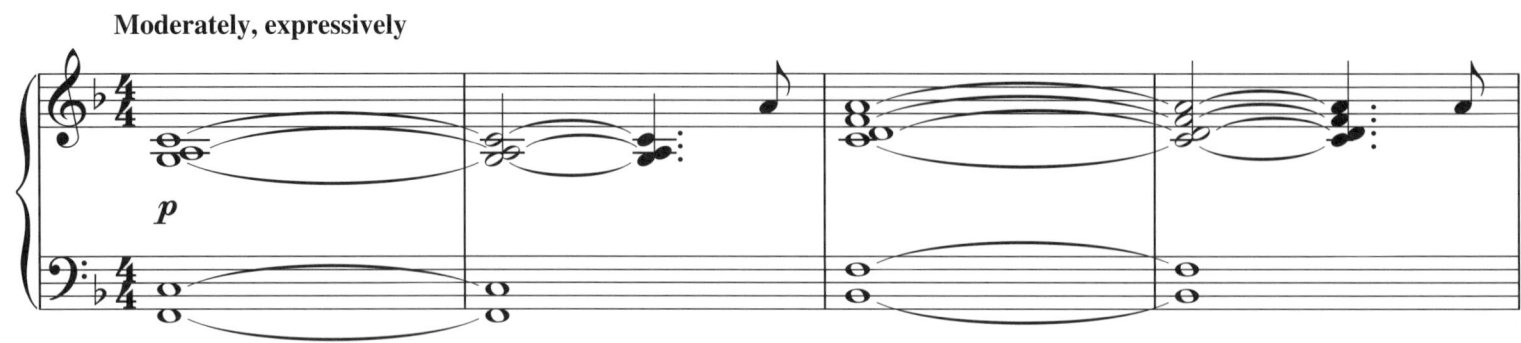

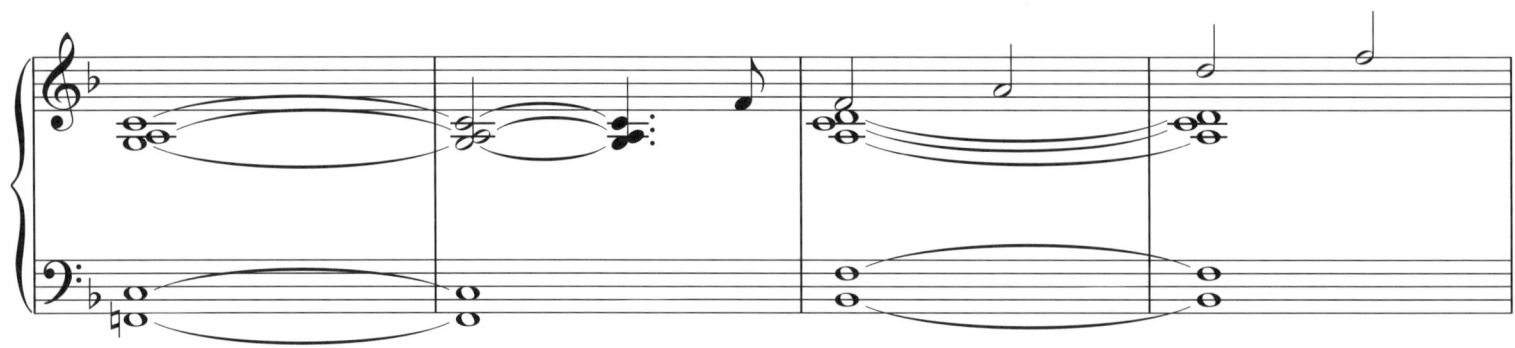

Copyright © 2010 by Moon Boy Music (BMI)
All Rights Reserved   Used by Permission